T4-AJW-713

SIGNS OF HOPE IN THE THUNDER OF SPRING

SIGNS OF HOPE IN THE THUNDER OF SPRING

BY ALVIN N. ROGNESS

ART BY DON WALLERSTEDT

AUGSBURG PUBLISHING HOUSE
MINNEAPOLIS, MINNESOTA

SIGNS OF HOPE IN THE THUNDER OF SPRING

Library of Congress Catalog Card No. 73-159009

International Standard Book No. 0-8066-1132-4

Manufactured in the United States of America

CONTENTS

PREFACE

Hope is the casualty of our day. Fear threatens to drive out hope for the future; and where hope is gone, love too is gone. A man cannot turn to a concern for his neighbor if he is paralyzed by fear. It is in an attempt to recover the basis of hope that these chapters are written.

This book is also the outcome of an invitation extended to me by Dr. Harold B. Kildahl, pastor of First Lutheran Church, Minot, North Dakota, to initiate a lectureship established by the First Lutheran Men entitled *The T. F. Gullixson Memorial Lecture Series.* On November 15-17, 1970, I gave the five addresses which, in content if not in precise form, are the substance of this book.

Thaddeus Franke Gullixson, for a score of years the pastor of First Lutheran Church in Minot before assuming the presidency of Luther Theological Seminary, Saint Paul, Minnesota, in 1930, was my teacher as well as my predecessor in office. I am grateful to the Men of First Lutheran for giving me the privilege of inaugurating this annual lectureship.

Alvin N. Rogness

CHAPTER ONE

I WANT COMFORT

I want comfort. There is no point ushering me into a world of anxiety and fear unless you first nestle me securely in the place of comfort.

I need a place of rest. There is no point dispatching a jet down the runway without first knowing its destination.

I want to know where I am going. There is no point letting the massive wheel begin to turn unless it is first balanced on its axis. Just to be in motion is not enough.

There are some big questions I want answered. Where did I come from? Where am I destined to go? What resources do I have to get there? What help may I look for on the way? What perils? Asking these questions is not enough. If I have no answers, I tend toward panic or paralysis or both.

There is nothing wrong in asking. Nor in having an open mind. Life is shrouded in mystery. Only the naive or the stupid have no questions. Only the fool has a closed mind. But everyone wants some answers—some big answers. Everyone wants some things settled, some solid place to rest. This is the comfort I demand.

Only the adventure of faith—faith in God—can usher in this comfort!

DOOMED TO GOD

Don't sell me short. I won't settle for trifles. You can't buy me off with a Cadillac and a three-level ranch house.

I'll take them, if they come my way, but that's not what I'm asking for. I want something more.

You've got me all wrong if you think life is made up of the security that stocks and bonds can give. And you've got the country wrong too if you think its gross national product is what makes it great.

I was made for God. That's where my trouble begins—and ends. I can't settle for less.

The clue to my trouble—and my comfort—is found in a strange story told in the Bible. God put me together to need him. He created me in his image, in his likeness. As he designed the fish to live in water and the birds to fly in air, so he designed me to live in and with him.

I might wish it were not so. I might very well want to go my independent way, neither troubled nor comforted by God. If I try it, my life ends in shallows and shambles. I have no option, really. If I want to live, really live, I've got to live in him. There's no other place to go.

Deep down in my being I want it that way. I want to need God, and I want God to claim me. It's the only way I can ultimately be of worth. It is the one key to human dignity. I want to be a *somebody*. I want to be important. I cannot have any sustaining comfort without it. To be of importance to God himself is the key to my humanity. Trying to understand myself without reckoning with this basic need will lead me into all sorts of blind alleys. I will chase phantoms in an endless and fruitless search for significance—and for comfort.

And there are all sorts of blind alleys to lure me.

The most pervasive and the most subtle temptation is to regard man simply as an animal. A very complex, often heroic, animal, but an animal nonetheless. He does amazing and terrible things. He writes oratorios and shatters cities with a blow. No other animal can match him.

It seems strange that he willingly identifies himself with the amoeba and the white rat, and takes his clue from them. He claims the chimpanzee as a cousin, and in a tragic way tries to understand himself within the narrow limits of biochemistry. But if he heads in this direction, he will blunder into one or more of three blind alleys.

THE DRIVE FOR SURVIVAL

The first is to understand himself primarily as an *eating* animal. The urge to survive is the elemental drive. Economics is the basic science. We need food. If we have enough to eat, and the assurance that we will continue to have enough to eat, we will be content. Give a man a full dinner pail and he will not strike. Keep a nation well-fed, and it will not go to war. Not only armies, but civilizations as well, move on their stomachs.

In this blind alley economic security is the highest good for the human being. Everything else about him is but frosting on the cake. He may strive for frosting too, like pretty clothes, elegant surroundings, charming companions—but it's the food on his plate that makes him tick.

Obviously a person needs food. Let him be without it for a few days, and he may be quite unpleasant. A symphony concert will not satisfy him. But the fact is that many of us, well fed, are still miserable, and not from gastric ulcers either. Nor is it true that the wealthy, those who have greatest assurance of the next meal, are the happiest segment of society. Karl Marx notwithstanding, man is more than an economic animal, and his need for food is not the profoundest clue to his humanity.

THE DRIVE FOR POWER

The second misleading clue is to understand man primarily as a *fighting* animal. He wants more than survival. He wants power, prestige, popularity. He is a competitor, satisfied only if he can receive the applause of his peers. To lose face is more distressing than to lose money.

This drive for power and approval is universal. Whenever it possesses a man, it plunges him into nasty competition with his brothers. And the appetite is never satisfied. He is not satisfied with second prize. Every achievement spurs him on to new and often ruthless rivalries.

It is unrealistic to underrate this drive. Each of us needs to excel in some way. If I cannot win in tennis, perhaps I can be the uncontested winner in checkers. I need some point in which I can excel.

But man needs to know how subtle and destructive the drive for power can be. If it becomes a pervasive appetite, it finally destroys itself. Power corrupts, says the philosopher, and absolute power corrupts absolutely. Power is too heady a drink. A person needs much grace to keep even a little power or popularity from dislodging him.

If we describe man in these terms, then politics—the science of power—becomes the chief study for man. Nations go to war not for economic reasons, but for political. For a nation to lose face is more serious than for it to lose a continent.

But if power or prestige were the highest good for man, if its achievement were the key to his true happiness, then Nero or Napoleon or Stalin should have been among the happiest of men. But they all ended in blind alleys.

THE DRIVE FOR SEX

The third deadend street lures man into believing that he is primarily a *mating* animal. Sex is the key to understanding him. Everything he does is a sublimation of this one overwhelming drive. Have him happily married, his glands functioning well, and he has fulfilled his destiny. Every rack of paperbacks today is eloquent witness to the wide acceptance of this premise.

During World War II a popular magazine published a study that suggested that if Adolph Hitler had not suffered an irregular sex life, he would have been a "nice" man and there would have been no war. History itself, on this premise, is but the long shadow of sex.

Again, it would be foolhardy to ignore the need to use sex properly. But to argue that man's life can be fulfilled only in terms of his glands is a caricature of everything we call human.

Each of these generalizations is limited because it begins with the supposition that man is no more than an animal. Complex and marvelous as he is, man is essentially no different from his lower cousins on the animal family tree. He may camouflage his drives in noble language, but they are as base and elemental as those of the tiger in the jungle.

We must take these drives seriously. And there is no advantage in renouncing our family connections with all organic life. Fortunately for us, we are related to the white rats. We can learn much about ourselves from a study of them. If this were not so, we would lose all the laboratory findings which our lower cousins have bequeathed to us. It would be highly ungrateful of me to be so haughty that I would not give homage to all these cousins who have been martyred in scientific laboratories for me.

But I do not derive much comfort, nor any sense of dignity, nor an awareness of great worth from arraying myself with the white rat, or even with the chimpanzee. They have very little capacity to endow me with importance. I am not a "somebody" because I belong to this family. The dignity of the guinea pig does not rub off on me.

THE TRAGIC HERO

And, frankly, I have trouble garnering any towering sense of worth by examining the performance of the human race itself. It should be possible to take inventory of the magnificent triumphs of science these past two hundred years and become rhapsodic over the achievements of the human family.

But I am melancholy. This twentieth century is marred by two major wars which have destroyed more people than the cumulative wars of all the centuries before it. Today the most powerful nation on earth spends a major part of its budget in arms, while its cities and countryside deteriorate. The conquest of smallpox, diphtheria, polio, and tuberculosis are offset by Hiroshima and Nagasaki. Hunger stalks two-thirds of the earth, while the planet's air and water are threatened by the very triumphs of technology.

Nor do I see any great surge of compassion encircling the globe. The exploding population tends rather to dehumanization, peoples and nations intensifying rivalries instead of brotherhood.

I try to remind myself that I am on the same family tree with an Einstein and a Pasteur, only to remember that I am also a brother of Hitler and Stalin. Great hospitals are built throughout the world at great cost, but costs that are minimal contrasted with the taxes required to punctuate the world with missiles that threaten potential suicide for the race.

If I am to derive comfort and a sense of worth by relaxing myself into the record of man's performance, ancient and modern, I find uneasy rest. In fact, I find no rest at all.

THE MOMENT OF TREMBLING

I come back to God.

It's a strange place to rest, to be sure. I have never

seen him nor touched him. There is no incontestable evidence that he exists at all. Nonetheless, this is where I find comfort. This is where my troubled spirit comes to rest.

Perhaps it is not strange after all. If I am created precisely to come to rest in him, then for me as a human being it is the most natural thing in the world. In fact, there is no other place for me to rest.

To come to terms with God, however, is not so easy. He is God. He sets the standards; he calls the shots. He judges the world, and he judges me. To come into his presence is not as casual a thing as dropping in on a friend for an evening.

Each of us appears before him to be judged, to receive a verdict, to be accepted or rejected. Fortunately for us, he has promised not to evict anyone who comes. But this does not mean that he does not judge. In coming to him, we come to terms with our sins and wretchedness.

The apostle Paul says, "But with me it is a very small thing that I should be judged by you or by any human court. I do not even judge myself. . . . It is the Lord who judges me."

No doubt Paul would not have dared to arraign himself before the high court of God if he did not already know the limitless mercy of that court. He recognized however that the verdict of men was often in error, also that his own self appraisal could be distorted. Only God has a right to give final sentence. Only God knows the hidden springs of the heart. But God knows. And this is both terrifying and comforting.

Terrifying as it is to appear before God totally stripped of any pretenses, I must appear. I need to be judged. I must have a verdict. To be passed over, to be dismissed as if I am not important enough to be judged at all, this is more frightening than being convicted.

To be adrift in the universe, unnoticed and unjudged, as if no one cares what I do or what I am—this is nihilism. "Set me free or send me to jail, but do not pass me by as if I am nothing." We need a God who judges us!

In Arthur Miller's *After the Fall,* Quintus, the attorney whose life was falling apart, says, "I think I have always thought of life as a case at law . . . my trouble began when one day I looked up and the bench was empty. There was no judge in sight. And life was an endless conversation with myself . . . a pointless litigation of existence before an empty bench—which is despair." Man cannot stand an empty bench. He needs to be judged, and by God! It is not enough to be judged by one's peers, or by history, or by oneself.

A boy of four was adopted after having been shuttled from one foster home to another. Two months later someone visited the home and the boy announced proudly, "My father spanked me." Someone loved him enough to judge him! This is the cry of the human heart—the cry for a God who cares enough to judge.

When in the parable of the Prodigal Son the son came back home, he said, "Father, I have sinned against heaven and against you, and am no longer worthy. . . ." He came back to a father who loved him and who would rightly judge him. The sequel of mercy which swept away the judgment does not destroy the fact that the father was rightly the judge, precisely because he was the father who loved him.

Man has always flirted with the fraudulent technique of minimizing and even destroying the difference between right and wrong, good and evil—in a sort of permissive world where anything goes. But he knows this is phony. Each of us knows that he must be judged. For God there are no gray areas. He alone can sort out right from wrong, good from evil. And, deep down, we yearn to get away from the lower courts (our fellowmen, ourselves) and appear before the only court that can give a just verdict, uncomfortable as that may be. We want to come clean, somewhere! Until that is done, there will be no comfort.

THE PLACE OF REFUGE

I remember punishing one of my boys. I think he was about three. When I had spanked him, he backed away from me, sobbing in anger and hurt and defiance. Suddenly he flung himself into my arms, clinging to me, sobbing still. He knew instinctively that the place of punishment was also the place of refuge. He who spanked was he who loved.

The God who judges is the God who saves. He who must sentence is he who has died on a cross to lift the sentence. This is the miracle of the gospel. This is the key to understanding God and his ways with us. In theological language, this is the strange fabric of law and gospel. Judgment is full and mercy is full. The law is not annulled; the law is fulfilled. Mercy is not cheap; it cost God a cross.

There is comfort in being judged. It is the guarantee that I am important. But the supreme comfort is in being given mercy; this is the guarantee that I am loved. If the heart of the universe is justice alone, I am undone. I dare not stand before the great God and ask that I be given what I deserve, no more no less, which is justice. If this is as much as I can hope for, I am in despair. My only cry is, "God, be merciful to me, a sinner." And the miracle is that there is mercy. The heart of the universe is love! Here I can rest. Now I know the one and only clue to comfort. Nothing can separate me from the love of God . . . in Christ Jesus.

Jonathan Edwards, the early American preacher, had a celebrated sermon entitled, *Sinners in the Hands of an Angry God.* This was a call to take God's holiness seriously.

Disturbing as this title is, this one–*Sinners in the*

Hands of a Loving God—may in a deep sense be more threatening. To face someone's anger is really not as frightening as facing someone's unrelenting love. I can return anger with anger—or with fear—and remain essentially unchanged. But to be loved and loved and loved—with a love that will not let me go—this threatens to melt the walls of my very being. Capitulating to this love, I will never be the same again. I become a captive to the one who loves.

Justice is never as strong as mercy. The law is power less to change me; the gospel is the key to an inner revolution so radical that it can only be described as a new birth.

Similarly, it is always more frightening to be the forgiven one than to be the forgiving one. Let us take the instance of two brothers, John and Robert, who have fought over their father's inheritance. For the past two years they have refused to talk to one another.

One day John comes to Robert's home, knocks at the door, and says to Robert, "Brother, I have come to ask for your forgiveness." In this instance, which of the brothers would you prefer to be?

I know which I would prefer to be. As Robert I would reply, "Forgive you? John, I am delighted to forgive you. I have waited these two years for a chance to forgive you. Why didn't you come to your senses long ago and admit you were wrong?"

And which of the brothers had undergone the great change? The forgiven one, the repentant one, of course. Robert could remain as priggish and proud as before. It was John who had invited the revolution, who had become "a new man."

As we meet the Lord who forgives and forgives, unendingly, "till seventy times seven," and understand ourselves as men and women who need a radical forgiveness—and who receive it from God, then we know ourselves as the forgiven ones and we grow as new creatures in Christ.

It is then that I have a place to stand. I stand upright, unafraid, as the restored child of God. I rest back into a universe which at its heart is love. I am still afraid, but with secondary fears—fear of cancer, unemployment, war. I now know that nothing, not even death itself, can separate me from God.

This is the comfort I have yearned to have.

CHAPTER TWO

GOD AND TOMORROW

Today I can manage. It's the tomorrows that get me down. Who knows what lies ahead? Only God knows. And he does not let me in on the future. I walk into the unknown.

I can know the past and the present. And I can also know that the past and the present somehow flow into the future. But there is always the unpredictable, the unexpected. I cannot be sure that the road does not have a sharp bend. I may suddenly find myself turned about, headed in an altogether new direction. This is the exhilarating hope—and sometimes fear—of God's world.

Trusting in God, how can I face my tomorrows? I cannot know what he may do, or what he might be able to do. After all, by giving us the freedom of choice, the right of independence, he has limited himself. We can thwart his will and his plans. In fact, we do it again and again. This is the awesome fact of existence. Had he made us puppets instead of self-determining beings, he could have had a world of no war, no violence, no injustice.

He is still God, however. He will have the last word. The ultimate victory over evil will be his. He has promised a new heaven and a new earth. The old order of sin and tragedy and pain and death will one day be over. In the meantime the course of history, mine and the world's, will be the interaction between a sovereign God who is free and mankind to whom he gave freedom.

This is what gives our tomorrows their unpredictable character. This is what gives to the future its fascination, its terror, and its hope of glory.

While recognizing that man with his perverse freedom can upset the plans of God, I am still unwilling to limit him. I believe that with God all things are possible, and that therefore anything can happen.

The last one third of this volcanic 20th century lies before us. We all have an irresistible urge to peer into the coming years in both fear and hope. What lies ahead for mankind? What sort of world will my grandchildren know before the century ends?

FROM OPTIMISM TO GLOOM

The century opened with almost unbridled optimism.

As early as 1910 Sir Norman Angel in *The Great Illusion* pointed out that in our modern world, interlocked as it is economically and politically, no nation could win a war. The victor and the vanquished alike would lose. And the implication of the book was that man was now too intelligent to wage war.

There was ground for optimism. Europe had not engaged in a major war for over a century. Bismarck had consolidated central Europe without bloodshed. In the United States the Civil War had been over for two decades and the country was bursting with progress.

Science had made great strides in medicine and technology. Each new discovery was hailed as another step in what was thought to be inevitable progress. Nothing could stop us from spiraling ever upward and onward. Day by day, year by year, we were getting better and better.

Darwin's *Origin of Species,* describing man's long evolution from the simple to the complex, from the primitive to the civilized, was a biological motif that was picked up by the philosophers and theologians and made to be the hope of man's moral journey. We were moving irresistibly from the beast to the angel, and there was nothing to stop us.

To be sure, there were voices of warning.

Already in 1918 Oswald Spengler's *The Decline of the West* pointed to an impressive index of signs which indicated that our proud civilization was in deep trouble.

But the Western world did not lose heart. Even World War I did not cool our ardor. When in 1917 the United States entered the war, it did so on the wings of two great slogans, "One war to end all wars," and "To make the world safe for democracy."

We slipped through the twenties with the dream still unsullied, despite the economic collapse at the end of the decade. But in the early thirties we were sobered. Kaiser Wilhelm had been defeated, but there were Stalin, Mussolini, and Hitler. Democracy had not been saved.

The war clouds were gathering. By the late thirties we were in the second great war. And when that war ended on those ominous punctuation marks at Hiroshima and Nagasaki, no one talked about having fought two wars to end all wars. Already we whispered our fears of a possible World War III which would end civilization for the West.

Meanwhile technology, the hopeful savior of mankind, was getting out of hand. The machine became both an asset and a liability. We had given up the naive faith that progress was "in the cards."

Franz Werfel describes the present mood in the allegory of the camel driver who is being pursued by his enraged camel. To escape, he leaps into a well. As he falls his clothes catch on a root projecting from the wall of the well. There he hangs, suspended. He looks up and sees the maddened eyes of the camel peering down at him. He looks into the bottom of the well and sees the fiery eyes of a dragon. And as his eyes become accustomed to the light, he notices two mice, one white and one black, taking alternate bites at the base of the root. A nasty situation!

Mr. Werfel says that man had hoped to be the driver of the machine, but the machine gone mad has turned on him and threatens to destroy him. At the same time he faces the prospect of some catastrophic death—the dragon. Meanwhile, time is running out, day and night—the white mouse and the black.

It is this heavy mood we find ourselves in, as we move into the last third of this century.

REAPPEAR GOD?

How will God deal with these remaining decades?

It would be presumptuous, even indelicate, to anticipate the ways of God. Whenever we attempt to defend him, we become comic characters. He needs no defense. We can neither dislodge him nor support him. We do not carry him; he carries us.

But there is nothing wrong with trying to assess man's stance over against God. Will we give God a chance to work his will with us? Are there signs of the times that give us hope that the dimension of "man's eternal spirit" will reappear? Can we hope that there will be a resurgence of those moral and spiritual qualities which can rescue man from his own destruction?

The first sign of hope is that we have given up some fraudulent faiths.

We no longer have faith in technology. Our knowledge explosion, so proudly hailed a few years ago, now hovers over us like a cloud. Is it filled with gentle rains or does it hide a tornado? When someone announces that the next ten years will see more advance in science than the last fifty, no one applauds. Science has already put into our hands instruments which we may not have the moral stamina to manage. Secular faith is gone. Where it once stood in such untarnished pride, there yawns a great emptiness.

We no longer have faith in automatic progress. We have given up Darwin as the key to utopia. History does not have built within it some *elan vital,* some resident force which drives man ever onward and upward. Man is a responsible being. God holds him accountable for the outcome of his own life and the life of the planet. He cannot rest on his oars and have the stream of history speed him on to some glorious harbor.

Nor do we have faith in the elemental goodness of man. Western Christendom forgot the biblical doctrine of original sin for a season. We looked on man as a budding angel instead of a suppressed beast. In the early 1900s we were quite sure that man could never again enact a Roman arena with its flow of blood, and then came Dachau.

At this moment the pendulum has swung dangerously far to the other extreme. We may have no hope at all for the human race. We may forget that he was made "a little lower than the angels." We may overlook the destiny that God has intended for us from the beginning. We may forget the bracing promise in Isaiah 40: "but they who wait for the Lord shall renew their strength; they shall mount up with wings like eagles, they shall run and not be weary, and they shall walk and not faint."

But the realism of crisis is better than the naivete of utopianism. Napoleon once said, "He who would be victor must know his enemy." We now know better than a century ago what the odds are. In our extremity, we are more likely to call on God. With the old phony faiths gone, we have a chance to turn to the kind of faith that will put us in touch with the immeasurable resources of God.

WHERE TO NOW?

There are signs that we are turning.

The emptiness left by the shattered faiths is itself a

symbol of hope. Historians describe the first century as "the fulness of time," a period when the ancient faiths had collapsed and a yawning abyss waited for some new faith to come. We now wait, not for something new, but for the true faith, overlooked and untried for a season, to surge forth again and water the dried and thirsting spirits of man.

The sensate age has run its course, declares Pitirim Sorokin in *The Crisis of our Age*. From the rediscovery of Greek culture in the Renaissance to the present, says Sorokin, man has steadily moved from the world of the spirit to the world of the senses. In the pre-Renaissance period man took seriously his role as a child of God, a creature of heaven; over ninety percent of his art was "celestial." Painters and sculptors worked with angels and saints as models. Music flowed into oratorios, requiems, glorias, Kyrie eleisons. But now, for six centuries, man has thought of himself as a child of nature, rather than as a being destined for eternity.

Already there is turn in the road. The sensate has exhausted itself in violence, in the pathological. Given enough time to avoid catastrophe, says Sorokin, man will emerge into the world of the spirit again. He will again believe that he is more than the cousin of the cockroach. He will reclaim his high station as a prince in a great, celestial kingdom.

Meanwhile, there will be orgies. Man will plunge into Dionysian debaucheries, in a riot of pleasures of the flesh. There will be drugs and alcohol, distorted sex, suicide, and violence. But this is the grim prelude to the death of the sensate age. Something new is around the corner. And this "something new" is the recovery of the old, old story of a God who loves, creates, redeems, and preserves man in a dignity that is eternal.

The current bizarre fad of astrology, palmistry, and other practices of the occult is a sign that man is reaching out beyond himself, individually and corporately, to find something or somebody that can do for him what he cannot do for himself. And perhaps in his blundering and fumbling search he will stumble upon God, who has all the while been hovering near in search of him.

THE EMERGING GUILT

We are accustomed to call our age the "permissive" age. Anything goes. The absolutes of right and wrong, good and evil, are gone. Ethics is governed by the concrete situation, the here and now. Ancient values are flung to the winds, and man must find his way without any moral guideposts along the road.

But, at this very moment, man is plagued by a sense of guilt more pervasive than at any time in the immediate past. At least in our Western society, we are more sensitive to the sins of omission than ever before. The hunger of the world, the injustices of the world, the homeless of the world—we cannot ignore any longer. Christ's judgment haunts us: "I was hungry and you gave me no meat. . . . I was sick, and you did not. . . . I was homeless and you did not. . . ." We can no longer rest content and innocent behind the curtained windows of our affluent comfort.

And who but God can deal with guilt of such magnitude? The word *sin* is inching its way into our life again with its attendant pain. And it is no longer sin over trifles. It now takes its real shape—the sin of self-indulgence, self-pity, the sin of indifference, the sin of lovelessness. It is the elemental sin of Cain who renounced any concern or responsibility for his brother. We can hide no longer. We have ignored our brother—our brother next door and our brothers the world over.

There may not be any obvious flood of love released among us, but never in many years are so many people uneasy over the absence of love in their lives and in the world. And this puts us within reach of him who alone is the source of love. "Repent, for the kingdom of heaven is at hand," was the evangelist's cry. The awareness of our neglects is at least a movement, however slight, toward repentance. We still have a long way to go until, with God's help, we can find ways to turn our backs upon our own self-indulgence to lift the burdens of the world. But I think we are on the way, and this is one of the most significant straws in the wind for hope in this weary 20th century.

APPLAUDING CHANGE

We tremble over the tempo of change. Things move too swiftly. Our technical genius makes us a mobile people. A new discovery, translated into industrial production, uproots whole communities in weeks. Institutions of long and venerable tradition and service seem suddenly inept, unable to cope with change. Universities, churches, governments, even family structures, come under fire. Especially our youth, facing the long years of responsibility, become critical of establishments that threaten to fail them.

We who are older share their fears, although perhaps with less poignancy because we do not have as many years at stake. And we may be a bit defensive of the institutions that we have shaped. But there is no gap in the quality of our anxieties.

Who is to say that change may not be to God's advantage? In his play, *A Sleep of Prisoners,* Christopher Fry has these striking lines,

> *The human heart can go to the lengths of God.*
> *Dark and cold we may be, but this*
> *Is no winter now. The frozen misery*
> *Of centuries breaks, cracks, begins to move,*
> *The thunder is the thunder of the floes,*
> *The thaw, the flood, the upstart Spring.*
> *Thank God our time is now when wrong*

Comes to face us everywhere,
Never to leave us till we take
The longest stride of soul men ever took.
Affairs are now soul size.
The enterprise
Is exploration into God. . . .

This may indeed be the outcome of God and our tomorrows. We may be on the verge of Spring. The pain of reshaping old forms, casting some aside, may be the birth pangs of a new and wonderful day for our poor earth. Our grandchildren may know an era far more golden than any in the world's history. We may be on the threshold of the recovery of God.

Nor do we dare to say that technology is not God's gift to us. These amazing advances in power and skill may be the very instruments God puts in our hands to make life take on a new goodness for his children. If he can be called in, if we can begin to manage his gifts according to the policies of his kingdom, think of all the tedium and cruel labor the world can be spared. At long last, we may be able to have the leisure required to see the beauties of the universe and to appreciate the rhapsodic possibilities of the spirit of man.

If—just if—all the energies and resources that have been devoted to war in this century were to have been directed to the domestic welfare of each country, think—just think—what sort of civilizations we might have had the world over.

Might we not be at the point in the long history of man when war will seriously be outlawed and abandoned as an instrument for settling our differences? Any show-down between the nuclear nations will now destroy us all. This fact has already produced a deadlock. Each great nation knows this is so.

We still roll on with gigantic military budgets—but with a growing sense of futility. Arms are no longer any guarantee of safety, or of victory, should they be used. How we will disentangle ourselves from this atomic snarl we are at a loss to know. But we know that it must be done. And this knowledge itself may be the beginning of having man turn to God. "Woe is me, I am undone," may become the cry of the whole world.

DARE WE LIMIT GOD?

However slender our hope is as we survey the enormous issues that face our world, can we who confess faith in God have any other stance toward our tomorrows than to entertain expectations of a better day? "If God is for us, who is against us?" said Paul, and "he that spared not his own Son, but gave him up for us all, will he not also give us all things with him?"

Our tomorrows simply cannot be a deadend street. The future is open-ended. We may not subscribe to the poet's exultant lines, "God's in his heaven—All's right with the world," but we can rest in the assurance that "the earth is the Lord's," and go on from there to believe that the Lord will not let his earth go without a struggle. He is on the side of the abundant life for his children, and he has resources far beyond our most extravagant calculations.

His strategy is to focus on the heart and will of a man. His revolutions always begin within man. He turns a man around, from fear to love, from indifference to mercy. He releases him from the prison cell of selfishness to roam in freedom the wide world of his brother's needs. He takes from him the fear of death and empowers him for the enterprises of life—life in justice and compassion for all men.

God invades and builds bridgeheads in the hearts of men. If he can have some bridgeheads here and there, whole communities and nations can change. These people become leaven and salt. They are the true nonconformists, the quiet revolutionaries that change the world. They are under higher orders. They love, because the love of God has captured them. They do not ask what the world can give them; they ask what they can give the world. Even when rebuffed, even when the odds seem too great for any success, they keep trying still.

In the north country nature seems most hopelessly dead in the last days of February, just before spring is ready to burst. It could be that our world is at this point, that imperceptible stirrings of the eternal spirit of man are already in motion, and that before the 20th century has ebbed away, a whole new epoch will have dawned for the children of men.

Every hope that we have is somehow anchored in God. He created us to be his own and to live with him here and hereafter forever. He sent his only Son to redeem the world and to usher in an imperishable kingdom. He who has begun this good work has promised to see it through.

And it must be remembered that we who lay such exorbitant claims to the love of God do not limit him to the narrow confines of this planet. If the planet blows up, and all of us in the twinkling of the eye are vaporized in a holocaust, this is not the end for us or for God. He has other holdings in his empire, and transportation facilities to put us to work again in another and better sector of his estates. We believe in the resurrection of the dead and life in the world to come.

This rapturous prospect does not lead us to abandon this earth, however. He has not abandoned it, nor can we. Future is horizontal as well as vertical. The Lord will come again in glory, but until he does, this earth is the arena where his great and wonderful will is at work in us and for us.

In one of the great galleries hangs a picture of Faust and the devil playing chess. Its title is *Checkmate*. The devil has Faust cornered, and sits leering at him. One day an old man stood long before the picture. Suddenly the corridor rang with his cry, "It's not true. The king has another move, the king has another move."

The King, our eternal King, will always have another move. The tomorrows are in his hands.

CHAPTER THREE

I NEED THE STORY

It's the greatest story ever told. And I need it. People have called it a fairy tale, a world of fantasy. Fantasy or not, I need it. I happen to believe that it is a true story, the kind of story that ties all of life together into some sort of epic. Without it, I find life fragmented, a thousand pieces in a jumble. Life remains a box of jigsaw pieces with no one putting it together.

It is in the Bible that the plot unfolds. The life, death, and resurrection of Jesus Christ form the center of the story, like the hub of a wheel. Like spokes of a wheel, the parts move toward and away from this one central motif.

The story itself—can it be true? Isn't it too good to be true? It promises too much. If it's true, it should change the world. And it would—if man would only let himself be caught up in it.

The history of man is his tragic unbelief. It's as if someone deposits a hundred thousand dollars in the bank to your account. The money is there. This is not fantasy. But you treat it as fantasy, and never draw a check. You are rich—vastly rich—but you live in poverty. Because you treat fact as fantasy! You do not live *as if* it is so.

Fact or fantasy, let's get on with the story. Let's forget about the first chapters for the moment. Let's start with the climax of the story—Jesus Christ!

He is the most tantalizing person who has ever lived

on this earth. By all historic precedents, he should long since have been forgotten. He should have been no more than a very local character in a small country long ago. Not a line should have been written about him. Once his peasant mother had died, no one should have remembered him.

THIS STRANGE MAN

After all, he had none of the credentials worthy of the historian's research. He was not rich, he was not learned, he belonged to no royal family. He was a carpenter's son in a small town. He became an itinerant preacher (there were many in those days), he attracted a small following (12 untutored men), and his life was snuffed out one Friday for disturbing the peace. That was all, measured by the usual canons of history.

For two thousand years he has haunted the world. Other great men have taken their quiet place in the shelves of libraries and no longer trouble the world—Alexander, Genghis Kahn, Nero, Napoleon. But not this Jesus of Nazareth.

Every other leader of men has had minor and local allegiances compared with him. Hundreds of millions of people throughout the centuries have lived and died for him. He simply does not fit in the long parade of the world's great. And today, in this 20th century, he bids to be the only candidate for the loyalty of the whole world. There is none other.

The church that bears his name is the most international movement of the day. The church does not win the applause of men everywhere. In fact, the church is under attack. But not the Lord of the Church. Pilate's verdict, "I find no fault in him," has been the unqualified verdict of the world ever since he lived among us. It is still the verdict of the world today. It was said of Gandhi, a Hindu, that he had but one picture on his wall—Jesus of Nazareth. The growth of the Christian movement has been largely westward from Jerusalem, it is true, but Jesus is the universal cosmopolitan. He is white, he is black, he is yellow. He belongs to all races and all time.

When in Lloyd Douglas' novel, *The Robe,* Marcellus, the Roman Captain, becomes Christian and is reviled for it by his friends, he asks, "If you are to choose one man to be the image of God, or to be God come to earth, what other candidate would you choose?" There is no other to rival him. He comes nearer to meeting the heart's desire than any other.

If any other part of the story is to become credible at all, we will have to let the life and person of Christ be the clue. He walked the earth. There are four biographies left to us: Matthew, Mark, Luke, and John. Read them. Read them as if you have never read them before. Let this man become your companion as you read. Imagine that you are there at his side as he talks with people and as he heals their hurts. Let the full force of his person strike you.

If you do, you will at least join Pontius Pilate in saying, "Behold, the man!" You may not initially echo the words of the centurion, "Truly, this man was the Son of God," but it will dawn upon you that if any man ever represented what man in the fullness of his humanity ought to be, Jesus was that man.

THE GLORY OF MAN

Now let us go back and begin where the story begins.

"In the beginning God created the heavens and the earth. . . . Then God said, 'Let us make man in our image, after our likeness.' "

So begins the history of man, his glory and his tragedy. God made him to be like God, with the gift of freedom, with the right of self-determination, with the terrifying gift of choice. Unlike all other creatures whose course was determined by inclination, disposition, and appetite, man alone was endowed with reason and will. Man could elect his course. He could choose good or evil. He could obey God or he could obey the enemy of God. He could climb the heights, or he could drift to the depths. He could build civilizations, or he could destroy them.

God could have made us to be puppets or automatons. He could have pulled the strings or pushed the buttons and spared us from war and disaster. He risked everything in having no strings to pull. His only pull was love. If he failed to reach us, capture us, and control us by love, the human enterprise was lost.

We will never understand the story at all if we do not grasp this one supreme fact. If love fails, all fails!

And love did fail. Man turned from the God who loved him and who destined him to the glory of eternal life with God. He turned to obey the enemy of God who despised him and who plotted to ensnare him in misery forever.

This is the villainous chapter in the story. It is sometimes called the Fall. The enemy lured man away from God, enticed him into his own clutches, and threw him into a vast concentration camp. There, away from God, man learned to love the darkness of the cell more than the light. His values were blurred and twisted. His desires were turned from the good and the noble to the base and the ignoble. He lost sight of the ultimate meaning of his life, and he was driven by his chaotic passions to all sorts of secondary goals. He lived in a misery which he could not understand. His proudest efforts turned to ashes. He had moved from life to death.

His estrangement from God was so complete that by his own imagination or effort he could not and would not have made the faintest gesture toward recovery. In the harsh language of Scripture, he was "dead in trespasses and sin."

In this state he would have remained forever—except

that God still loved him. This is the incredible dimension of God's love. He would not let man go. God immediately put in motion a maneuver to recover him. He promised a Savior! And in the fulness of time he sent him, his only begotten son.

YOU CAN'T STOP HIS LOVING

We who understand something of love, how can we comprehend either the quality or the scope of this kind of love? It is a love that gives and gives and gives, however often and much it is rebuffed or despised.

This love is different from anything else that we may know as love. A tiger in the jungle defends her cub, a mother has compassion for her child, a man for his friend. I may even pity my enemy. These "natural" compulsions I sometimes call love. These are not divine love.

It is natural for me to love the lovely, to be attracted to the attractive. The love God has reached out to love the unlovely, to be attracted to the unattractive, and by the sheer power of this love to transform the unlovely into the lovely.

I may love someone because of the possibilities I see. A teacher has a boy in her class who is incorrigible. He is mean, stubborn, unresponsive. But she sees possibilities in him. She lavishes her concern upon him, her patience stretched to the limit. If after months of effort, he remains as unattractive as ever, she will give up, perhaps regretting that she ever bothered with him. If God would have loved us because of our possibilities, how long since would he not have given up on the human race? After almost two thousand years of the reign of the Prince of Peace, the nations that bear his name in this century have engaged in two gigantic wars, more devastating than all the cumulative wars of history.

The love of God (agape) is something quite different. It is unconditioned love. It stops at nothing. You can't stop God from loving you, do what you will, any more than you can stop the sun from shining. You may pull the blinds and keep the sun from reaching you, but you can't stop the sun from shining. It is so with the love of God. I can turn from him, shut the door of my heart on him, keep him at bay. He will not force the door. He only keeps knocking. I can keep his love from ever reaching me and spend an eternity away from him. This is the awesome power he has given me by giving me the gift of freedom.

HISTORY'S MOMENT

"But when the time had fully come, God sent forth his Son, born of a woman, born under the law, to redeem those who were under the law, so that we might receive adoption as sons."

Why did God wait so long? Why did he let century after century go by before he sent Jesus? There is no clear answer. The Bible tells how God singled out Abraham and his family (the Israelites) to carry the promise of a savior, how he groomed them generation after generation in times of faithfulness and in times of apostasy.

The prophets of this nation kept reminding their people of the great day to come, when the Messiah would arrive. They became a people of promise, who lived day by day in the expectation of that which was yet to come. There were clues of what he would be like: "he has borne our griefs and caried our sorrows . . . he was wounded for our transgressions . . . he was bruised for our iniquities . . . with his stripes we are healed." He would be a sorrowing, suffering Lord. There would be a cross as well as a crown.

It was not easy for this small nation, harried and oppressed again and again by their more powerful neighbors, often in exile—it was not easy for them to understand this Messiah in any other light than that of a great warrior, an emancipator who would forever rid them of their oppressors.

When finally the savior came as a child in Bethlehem and as a peasant from Nazareth, most of the people found him a great disappointment. They regarded him as a dreamer, a fraud. They rejected him and let him die on a cross at the hands of the Roman soldiers.

That should have been the end. But he rose from the dead, and the story went on. In fact, it gathered momentum, until in three short centuries it dominated the Mediterranean world. The Messiah had indeed come. God had visited his people on the earth. The great maneuver of recovery and reconciliation had been executed.

To believe in a savior who was to come may really be no more difficult than to believe in a savior who has come. To accept Jesus Christ as Lord in retrospect may require the same kind of faith as to accept him in prospect. The whole story, from beginning to the end, demands faith. The ancient Israelites lived by promise. I still live by promise by the Word of God which challenges me to stake my life on the staggering implications of this story, and his promise that if I do, I will not be betrayed.

It is an exciting venture, and the stakes are incredibly high. It is as if I were to ask myself: "This story may be true, or it may not be true. But—and this is the crucial issue—will you have it be true if it can?" And from the depths of my bewildered, inquiring, groping, hoping spirit, I answer, "With all my heart I want it to be true."

Because if it is indeed true, there are some magnificent corollaries that follow. Then there is a God who loves me. I am not left marooned, alone and comfortless, in these swift years on the planet. I am really *somebody*. I am a son of God, a child in the most royal family in the universe. I have title to a kingdom which death itself cannot touch. My sins are forgiven. I stand before the great God of the universe, acquitted, victorious—an heir of God.

At the very moment when I am harried by guilt, overcome by fear, crushed by failure, I can say, "No matter, I am still a child of God, cradled in his strong and gentle arms."

THE GREAT PICTURES

The story goes on to tell what Christ accomplished in his 33 years on earth. Three great pictures emerge in the Scriptures.

The first is the *window*. In Jesus Christ we see God. The universe opened for a moment and revealed what God is like. No longer do we echo the melancholy words of Robert Ingersoll at his brother's grave: "Life is a narrow vale between the cold and barren peaks of two eternities. We try in vain to look beyond the heights. We cry aloud, and the only answer is the echo of our wailing cry. From the voiceless lips of the unreplying dead there comes no word."

We have more than an echo. We have a Word from God, a Word made flesh. Jesus of Nazareth we confess to be "God of God, Light of Light, Very God of Very God." If we want to know what God is like, we point to Jesus Christ. In him and through him we know that God is a God of infinite love. He is not a weary monarch, a cruel tyrant, an immovable judge. He is a great and good father. He is a sorrowing, comforting, healing brother. He is a merciful friend.

The second picture is a *battle field*. Man is overcome by hostile and evil forces, within him and without. Life is too much for him. He cannot win the battle with his own resources. Generation after generation he faces defeat. But he is not on the field alone. His brother, Jesus Christ, the only son of God, has invaded the earth, has engaged the enemy, Satan, and has overcome him. The decisive battle was fought on a knoll outside of the gates of Jerusalem—on a cross. In some strange and wonderful way beyond our knowing the dominion of the enemy was broken. We were set free from his clutches. The doors of his prison were shattered, the doors to the father's house were flung wide, and we were free to leave the darkness of our cells and return to the blazing glory of the palace.

But Jesus died that day on a cross. How could he, in death, be the victor? The story takes a strange turn. He had come to die. It was his purpose, and the purpose of God. It was by his death that he would release us from everlasting death. The enemy had tried again and again to deflect him—to keep him from dying. Three times in the wilderness he had tried to distract him. At the cross, in the raucous taunts of the crowd, "If you are the Son of God, come down," he had hoped to break him.

This event of long ago at Golgotha became the decisive battle in mankind's war against all that is evil.

When the Nazi forces were defeated in Central Europe in the mid-forties, the small nations, Belgium, Holland, Denmark, Norway, suddenly found themselves free again. They did not win the battle. A greater power in another part of the continent had won the battle. But this victory by another made them free. Their oppressors were still there, but their power was broken. No longer did they need to take orders from them.

Over nineteen hundred years ago a dying man cried, "It is finished," and a whole world was set free.

A third picture is the *court room.* Man faces the high court in judgment. He has no chance. In the presence of a court that demands perfection, man with his sins and guilt has no recourse. He must fling himself on the mercy of the court. When he does, he discovers a most radical turn. The judge descends from the bench, takes man's sentence upon himself, and pays the penalty of death for him. The innocent takes the guilt and punishment of the sentenced one, and the guilty one receives the righteousness of the innocent one.

This picture may offend us. This is a wanton miscarriage of justice. It is unfair; it is indecent. It destroys the very structure of law. It ignores the elemental moral world, where the offender deserves to be punished. It violates every ethical order in letting the innocent be punished for the guilty

But behind the cold transaction in the court room lies the warm and passionate love of a God who is at once judge and redeemer. He must judge, otherwise justice itself would be meaningless. But he must save, because he is a great father who loves.

Do with these pictures what you will, but behind them lies the towering theme of the story itself. God loves—with radical, unlimited, and everlasting love.

God came to this earth in Jesus Christ to *do* something for us that needed to be done. He did not come on a quick visit, a casual holiday, a reconnaissance flight. He came to become one of us, in order that we again might be one with him. It cost him a cross.

GRACE ALONE

We miss the genius of the story if in any way at all we limit the love that God has for us. Sometimes a mother may say to her child, "If you do this, mother won't love you." Either she is lying, or she does not have the love of a mother.

God does not say, "If you do this or do not do that, I will not love you." Remember, you cannot stop him from loving you, no matter what you are or what you do. If you forget this, you have not really understood the story.

Suppose a bee should return to the hive and say, "I've made a great discovery. Man loves us. It does not matter whether we sting him or not, whether we give him honey or not—he loves us still, just because we are bees." Obviously, its report is false. If the bee gives me no honey and if it stings me, I have no affection whatever for it.

But the story is just such a report. God loves me, whether I do his will or not, whether I hurt him or not. He loves me still. This is the key to the understanding of what the Bible calls grace. I am accepted by him, justified, not by my works or by performance, but by grace through faith alone.

But don't make the mistake of calling this cheap grace. I am received by God "just as I am, without one plea . . ." to be sure. But having come back to him, having found myself as a son in his kingdom, understanding in some small way the love that brought me there, there will be a thousand gentle but terrifying pressures to live like a son. I risk never being the same person again. Why not? I don't want to be the same person. I want to know the excitement, the glory, the height and depth of what it means to be a child of God, and thus to be fully a human being.

THE ETERNAL EPIC

A teacher in high school told me that a good story would have five parts: introduction, rising action, climax, declining action, and conclusion. This story has only three. There is the introduction: God made me in his image to live with him forever. There is the rising action: the enemy lured man away from God, and God in response put in motion a plan for his recovery. There is a climax: in the fullness of time God invaded the earth in Jesus Christ, his son and now my brother, and he died on a cross and rose again to become my savior.

At this point in the story there is no declining action and no conclusion. The sweep of the story keeps going up and up. I am caught up in the life of the kingdom. I am involved in the reconciling work of God on this earth. Every person becomes my brother. Management of the planet is restored to me. Every part of the world—every phase of life, every institution, every relationship—will come under the pervasive policies of God's kingdom.

There simply are not hours enough and years enough. Life is full. Even its sorrows, pains, and failures are swallowed up in the story that now has become an integral part of the story of my own life.

I don't know how many years may be given me. I may not have even one more day. But until the end I have a significant job to do. Whether I am formally employed or unemployed matters little. The big job, the overarching commission, is still mine. I am a son of God—to do his will in every concrete situation that meets me. Even on a bed of pain, with a terminal illness facing me, I have the high privilege of meeting pain and suffering as a child of God, spreading what cheer I can in the swift days left to me.

The planet itself is on impermanent tenure. I know he will come again one great day to usher in the fullness of his kingdom.

Death has lost its sting. It now is but a punctuation mark, a comma in the breathless story that has no ending, not even in eternity.

I need this story. I need it desperately. The lessons of history are not enough to brace me for the probable storms with hope. A survey of the triumphs of science and technology is not enough. If I am to assume management of my own life and the life of the world with any zest and confidence, I must have the assurance and the guidance that comes from this, "the old, old story, of Jesus and his love."

CHAPTER FOUR

THE WAYS OF GOD

In his celebrated poem, *Paradise Lost,* John Milton approaches his epic task with this prayer:

> *What in me is dark*
> *Illumine, what is low raise and support;*
> *That to the height of this great argument*
> *I may assert Eternal Providence*
> *And justify the ways of God to men.*

Milton was too audacious. How can any human being justify the ways of God to man? And is it not almost blasphemy to try? Does God need, or want, an attorney for the defense?

The best we can do is to describe his ways, as we have discovered them in Scripture and in experience—our own and the experience of worshiping people throughout the centuries.

Psalm 2 tells of people who presume to be attorneys for the prosecution, people who set out to dislodge God from his throne. "He who sits in the heavens laughs," says the Psalmist. "The Lord has them in derision."

Even to presume to describe his ways is a task to cause trembling. I approach the prospect with great caution. And God cautions me. "My thoughts are not your thoughts, neither are your ways my ways . . . . For as the heavens are higher than the earth, so are my ways higher than your ways and my thoughts than your thoughts."

But if I am to have any traffic with God at all, I must

try. How does he deal with me? This becomes the most important question in all existence for me, far more important ultimately than how you may deal with me, how my government will deal with me, or how my age will deal with me.

From the earliest recollections of my childhood I have known God as a God of infinite mercy who in Christ forgives my sins and arrays me before him as if I had never sinned at all. It is only as I rest my case in this staggering truth that I have even the courage to think about his ways at all.

However much I may be swallowed up in his mercy, I know also that I am accountable to him. He is my judge. I have other judges. You, for instance. Also, I am a kind of tribunal for myself.

The Apostle Paul summarizes the courts to which I come for judgment: "I for my part care little about being examined by you or by any human court. I do not even offer myself for investigation. For while my conscience does not trouble me at all, that does not prove that I am innocent. It is the Lord who must examine me." In Paul's description, there are four courts.

First, you. My contemporaries judge me. This is the lowest court, and the one which I should fear the least, and often the one I fear the most. "What really do you think of me?" It is the lowest court because it is the one which makes the most mistakes. Socrates, for instance, was accused by his fellowmen of corrupting the morals of the Athenian youth and was sentenced to drink the hemlock. History has reversed the decision and has pronounced him one of the greatest of ancient ethical men. John Huss was burned at the stake for heresy, and history has given this Bohemian a place among the immortals of those who championed truth. And Joan of Arc died on the fagots for treason, and later France has elevated her to the station of savior of her country. And Jesus himself! "Crucify him, crucify him," shouted the court! Think of the two thousand years of reversal of that verdict.

And yet I tremble before this court, so often wrong. I worry about what people will say. I fawn over the jury to get a favorable verdict. I want acceptance so badly. I yearn for popularity with such eagerness that I lose sleep when I think someone does not approve of me.

The next court is history, the future. When I am dead and gone, when people have had a better chance to assess me dispassionately, when more of the facts and the evidences are in, then a more sober verdict may be given. But even this court can err. Marc Antony offered this cynical observation in his eulogy of the dead Caesar:

The evil that men do lives after them,
The good is oft interred with their bones.

Even this court may miss. To be sure, many of the names that make the headlines today—rock singers, athletes, and others—will be forgotten, and some obscure Pasteur or Einstein will fill pages in history books. But think of the truly great, some mother or some humble friend, who may go unnoticed by both courts.

Then there is my own verdict on myself. I know myself better than you do. It is a solemn thing to take matters before my own heart or conscience. I try not to do this. I may trick you, I may even deceive history, but I have a harder time with myself. I may walk away from the ovations of the crowd with a heavy heart or with a sense of shame at having deceived them, simply because I cannot get a confirming verdict of approval in my own conscience

Paul says that he does not trust this court because he has trouble making any sort of case against himself. He concludes, "It is the Lord who must examine me." After all, only he knows the inner recesses of the heart, the deep inner motives that govern us. And so we come to the fourth and last court. It is terrifying to face this

all-knowing court. But it is also therapeutic. There is something cleansing in being stripped of all pretenses, all defenses, to be thrown totally at the mercy of the court with the cry, "God, be merciful to me, a sinner."

Only as we stand before the high court do the other three courts lose their grip on us. To be able honestly to say that we care far less about what other people think than what God thinks of us—this is a profound emancipation. We are free of some of life's fiercest and most phony tyrannies.

ENTER MERCY

Judgment and mercy, the law and the gospel, accountability and freedom are the poles between which I find myself. I find myself there because I know God as both judge and savior. He is a great and good Father. On the one hand he judges and punishes—in love—and on the other hand he goes to the lengths of a cross—again in love—to rescue and save

Mercy would have no significance were there no sin and judgment to make mercy necessary. The gospel, the glad good news of forgiveness, would have no meaning were it not that I stand guilty and undone without pardon. Accountability would be a fiction were I not a responsible being who had been given anew by grace the gift of freedom.

But there is mercy, there is forgiveness, there is freedom. These are the towering gifts that God as a father, and as a brother in Christ, has offered me.

"If thou, O Lord, shouldst mark iniquities, O Lord, who could stand? But there is forgiveness with thee." This is the key. He does count iniquities, he does judge. But there is forgiveness. There is a cross.

He could not possibly be a God of love if he did not judge, if he never bothered to hold us responsible. As a father of six children I would have been not only a poor disciplinarian, but a father derelict in love if I had simply overlooked their wrongdoing. If on the other hand I were no more than a vigilant policeman, making sure that every infraction earned its just punishment, I would be less than a father.

It is difficult for me to live in the tension which this dual role of God creates for me. But I must. It is the only chance I have to understand the ways of God with me. I must never cease to tremble before his judgment. I must never cease to rest in the overarching mercy of his love. If I lose either, I lose God.

On the one hand I face the temptation of making a case for myself over against God the judge, and in consequence having no need of mercy. On the other hand, I may bask in such relaxed ease over against his mercy that I lose altogether the need for obedience and discipline.

THIS UNSUCCESSFUL DEFENSE

I have an almost irresistible urge to defend myself. I do not like to be without any case whatever as I face God. I may present some favorable verdict of the three lower courts as evidence. After all, people like me. Moreover, I have some achievements that will stand the test of the future. And I can honestly say that I am satisfied with some of my performance. To have this comprehensive brief disallowed in God's court seems unjust. There must be a way to justify myself in some little way. But in the mysterious and magnificent ways that God has in dealing with me, he cannot allow it. He insists that I be thrown totally on the mercy of the court.

Søren Kierkegaard has an essay in which he points out how exhilarating it is that over against God we are always in the wrong. Suppose for an instant that I could be right and God could be wrong.

Suppose that a husband is told that his wife no longer

loves him, that she has fallen in love with another and is seeing him secretly. He does not believe it. But the rumor begins to haunt him. He can't sleep. He can't do his work. He begins to see in everything she says and does, or in everything she does not say or do, evidence of her faithlessness. In this situation, which would he like to be, right or wrong in his suspicions. Would he like to find it true? Would he like to be the one to forgive? How wonderful if he discovered that the rumor was utterly false, that all his suspicions were unfounded, that properly understood every evidence of her unfaithfulness was in fact evidence of her love. How wonderful that he could be wrong and she right, and that he would have to ask her forgiveness for his distrust.

God has *given* me the right to be his, with no strings, no conditions. I need not win the right; I need only accept it. D. T. Niles, the great evangelist from Ceylon, said that we are all beggars inviting other beggars to the feast. We have no claim, but we have the invitation. Why worry about defending our rights when the kingdom is ours?

George Macdonald, the great Scottish preacher who profoundly influenced the life of C. S. Lewis, speaks of rights:

> *Lest it should be possible that any unchildlike soul might, in arrogance and ignorance, think to stand upon his rights against God, and demand of him this or that after the will of the flesh, I will lay before such a possible one some of the things to which he has a right. . . . He has a claim to be compelled to repent; to be hedged in on every side: to have one after another of the strong, sharp-toothed sheep-dogs of the Great Shepherd sent after him, to thwart him in any desire, foil him in any plan, frustrate him of any hope, until he come to see at length that nothing will ease his pain, noth-*

ing make life a thing worth having, but the presence of the living God within him.

It is God's purpose to bring a man to bay, to have him stand helpless before him, to have his proud independence shattered, to have life become meaningless, to have him cry out for help, for comfort, for mercy. Until this happens, man cannot exult in the length and breadth, height and depth, of the love of God. Man is on a teeter-totter. If he is way down in his own need on the one side, he can be way up in his gratitude to God on the other side.

Harry Emerson Fosdick, one of the great preachers of our century, in his later years declared that the first third of our century had misled men in their optimism. We had become overconfident, smug in our achievements. In consequence, we had relegated God to "the chairmanship of the board," a sort of benign presence whom we really did not need for the central executive tasks of life.

We are smug no longer. The last third of our century sees man at long last looking beyond himself for help. This is true of us corporately as technological men. It is true of us individually as moral creatures.

THE OFFENSE OF THE CROSS

But we do not give up easily. In fact, there is something ignoble, something indecent, in throwing in the sponge. We are responsible beings, and should be held accountable. There should be no easy way out.

A friend of mine called me to say that he had just been to his doctor. The diagnosis was cancer. He had six months to live. He said, "I am not afraid to die, but I am afraid to meet God. You've got to help me. How does he deal with me?"

I tried to tell him that God dealt in mercy, that God

in Christ forgives and regards man as if he had never sinned. I remember how he recoiled at this. He was trained in jurisprudence, and this seemed utterly wrong. How could God treat a guilty one as if he were innocent? This would destroy justice. It would make mockery of law. He said, "I have never believed in purgatory, but I know he has to clean me up before he can let me in."

When I went on to talk about the mystery of the cross, his trouble deepened. How could God assign the guilt of the human race to One who was altogether righteous? What travesty! To let the guilty one off was bad enough. But to transfer the sins to one who was without sin and let him take the penalty—this would make shambles of everything. "The lowest court in the land would not deal in such miscarriage of justice," he retorted.

I knew now what the apostle Paul meant by "the offense of the gospel." The law is not offensive. Anyone with an ounce of decency will recognize that the guilty should be punished and the innocent acquitted. We move completely out of the world of justice into the world of mercy. The cross of Jesus is that world.

His sense of jurisprudence notwithstanding, the Holy Spirit broke into his heart and ushered him into this new and strange world. And when it happened, it was as radical an awakening as if it had happened to a Roman patrician in the first century. The strange ways of God with us are always like that.

A contract is always "You do this and I will do that." God says, "You do nothing. I do all." This is the way of radical love. The nearest parallel we have in human experience is probably that of a great and good mother. A mother of ten children was asked, "Which of the ten do you love the most?" She smiled, "I love them all, but I suppose at any given moment I love him most who needs me the most."

THE BIRTH OF GRATITUDE

What really is at stake is gratitude. How does a man become deeply grateful to God, and in his gratitude turn to give his life to God and his ways? Can he plumb the depths of gratitude if God and he are on a 50-50 basis with God saying, "You do half and I'll pick up the other half"? Or even on a 99-1 basis? Will not man cling to the 1% in pride, and lose the rhapsody of gratitude?

The biblical truth, "grace alone," emphasizes the strange jealousy of God. He *wants* to do it all. He maneuvers us into the position where he must do it all. Everything we are, everything we achieve, everything we hope for—everything is given us. We are indebted for the staggering gift of all of life.

I cannot keep my heart beating the next minute on my own. I cannot keep my brain in balance, prevent it from slipping cogs, on my own. I have absolutely no control of the network of the future on my own. I am a totally dependent being. I am a responsible being, to be sure, but I am still a totally dependent being, however contradictory this may seem.

A foolish "consistency is the hobgoblin of little minds," says Emerson, and if we are to grasp in some little way the style of God, we will have to abandon consistency. This is not the world of the logician. It is the world of the poet, the world of the man of faith. It is nonetheless a real and valid world. Its truth is confirmed in the lives of hundreds of millions of people.

God demands all. God gives all. This is the mystery! This is the law and the gospel.

James speaks of the "law of liberty." We have been set free from the law and its condemnation. We are ushered into a new, an utterly new world. It's a heady drink. Our sins are forgiven, our guilts no longer haunt us. We are free at last. Free from the guilt of sin, free from the dominion of sin. We are restored to the Father's house as sons and daughters. We may not look like sons or act like sons, but we are restored sons through the miracle of the work of the only begotten son for us. This is the "old, old story of Jesus and his love."

Can anything in all the universe compare with this? We are freemen again, free in the glorious house of our eternal and heavenly father. We are in his house, engulfed by the ways of his house, companioned by him and other restored children, recommissioned to the tasks of sons of the house. The pressures of a kingdom are upon us. Our old ways are threatened, because they are alien to this new world. They do not fit. Self-indulgence, self-pity, self-concern, self-accusation—none of these belong in this new order.

In a dream a man found himself at a long table. Every person at the table had his arms in slats, from the shoulder down to his wrist, as if the elbow were broken. The table was laden with food. But no one could bend his elbow to feed himself. Each sat immobile, looking in famished desire at the food, unable to reach it. Suddenly one began feeding his brother across the table, and his brother in turn began to feed him, until the entire table was one grand feast of brother feeding brother.

The strange ways of the kingdom are reflected in this dream. Not by necessity, however, but out of gratitude. I turn to my brother as the only way in which I can thank God in a concrete way. He has given the clue, "Whatsoever you do to the least of these, you have done it to me."

But I do it out of gratitude. This is the miracle of the kingdom. It is not simply that I must interest myself in others in order to survive. Survival as a goal is never enough. It never ennobles. It is when man turns to his brother out of love (because God first loved him), quite apart from whether concern for the brother will promote survival or not—it is only then that life will take on a touch of the divine.

THE ONE GREAT CLUE

How do you know that God loves you? There is no clear answer apart from the cross.

> I know not how that Calvary's cross
> A world of sin could free;
> I only know its matchless love
> Has brought God's love to me.

You cannot know the love of God in the sun that shines or the rain that falls. The sun may burn to a crisp the growing grain, and no farmer in his right mind would get up in the morning to an unclouded sky and say, "God loves me because he lets the sun shine." The rain may swell into floods and sweep men and beasts to their death, and in that moment no one would say, "God loves me because he lets the rains fall."

You cannot know the love of God in the variant circumstances of your life. Cancer may rob a child of its mother, despite all the prayers that have been prayed. There is no evidence, no clear evidence, except in this strange event of the cross. Over nineteen hundred years ago, on a knoll outside of the city gates of Jerusalem, a carpenter's son died on a cross between two thieves. Millions of people in every century since have looked to this cross as God's shining evidence that he loves man with an everlasting love. For God was in Christ reconciling the world to himself. And he loved man to the death, his own death. "Greater love has no man than this, that he lay down his life for his friends . . . you are my friends."

Our eyes turn back across the centuries, therefore, away from the flux of our daily plight, or the plight of the planet in the twentieth century, to fix our gaze on the supreme witness of God's love—the cross.

In the life, death, and resurrection of one Jesus of Nazareth, the world has been inspired to affirm the everlasting love of God. Resting in that love, men have turned to the day-by-day tasks of life with the glow of eternity in their hearts. They see in their brothers the God whom is gratitude they want to serve.

CHAPTER FIVE

GIVE ME A TOMORROW

I'm glad for the yesterdays and for the gift of memory to contain them. Their joys and sorrows weave a rich pattern. But I want a tomorrow.

Never in my lifetime have the tomorrows been so hard to claim. From every media of communications I am warned that there may be no tomorrows. Man's very existence on the planet is in jeopardy.

What am I to do? A venerable scholar, grown cynical, announced that if he were now 20 he would throw it all up and turn to drugs and fornication. A few are doing just that. But most of us, young and old, yearn and long for a future, a future with many of mankind's ancient enemies overcome—hunger, poverty, injustice, war. It is more a wistful longing than a strident one. But we have not sounded retreat. We move toward a tomorrow, hesitant and fearful though we may be.

The future we hope for is always a mixture of a recovered yesterday and a new tomorrow. "The good, old days" are in themselves not good enough. We press toward something yet to be.

Within the religions and cultures of many people there are the stories or legends of a glorious past. In the recovery of the past often lie the hopes for the future. Certainly within the Christian faith we affirm this truth. In the first chapters of Genesis we are given the epic of a magnificent beginning. God created all things and declared it all good.

Then came the tragic chapter. Man separated himself from God, and became the victim of long centuries of pain and suffering and death

The sixty-six books of the Bible are an account of recovery. God did not leave man to go his separated way unmolested. God intervened. He wanted man to have again the life which he had intended for him from the beginning.

LOSS AND RECOVERY

What really did Adam and Eve lose through disobedience and separation? What precisely is it that we must recover if our tomorrows are to be joined to the glories of the past?

I am intrigued by Genesis 3:7. "And the eyes of them both were opened and they knew that they were naked. . . ." Why were they not aware of their nakedness before the fall? A child of two is not aware of nakedness. He will toddle into a crowd stark naked and feel no embarrassment. The mother may be embarrassed, but not the child. Why? The child has not yet developed self-consciousness. He is totally absorbed in the world of people and things around him. Even when he plays with his toes, it is as if his toes belong to another world.

Perhaps this is the key to the bliss of Eden. Adam and Eve were completely lost in the wonder and awe of things and people outside of themselves. They had no temptation to self-indulgence, self-pity, self-accusation, self-concern. Their lives were caught up in three centers, three foci.

First, God. They were captured by the greatness and goodness of God. They rested back into his care with no trace of distrust. They took him for granted as they took for granted the sky above them. Wonder and awe and gratitude filled their hearts.

Second, they were fascinated by the beauties of the

Garden. Everything was theirs to enjoy. The beauties of color, form, and music enthralled them. They walked through the Garden as possessors.

Third, they were absorbed in each other, Adam in Eve and Eve in Adam. They lived in the innocence of lovers that ask nothing of each other but give to each other with gladness and mirth.

In one tragic moment they lost all three centers. They hid from God, and they lost him. They were driven out of the Garden to become fugitives in the earth. They turned in upon themselves and lost each other, as evidenced in Cain's cynical retort to God when he had murdered his brother Abel, "Am I my brother's keeper?" God, the Garden, and the brother were all lost. Man turned in upon himself as the one focus, and his long history has been one continuous preoccupation with self. This is his sin, his tragedy, and his hell.

If I am to have any tomorrow worth having at all, I will need to move toward the recovery of these centers of life. To the extent that I can again be lost in wonder and awe over the goodness and greatness of God, to the extent that I can again possess the earth as a Garden to care for and to enjoy, and to the extent that I can turn from myself to my brother—to this extent will my tomorrow be a renewal of all that which the Lord had destined for me

I will never be whole without this recovery. Without it, anything else I may find in the future will doom me to disappointment. "What has a man lost, if he has lost the whole world, but kept his soul?" It is this quality of life which is the highest good. Edwin Markham's poem expresses the issue well:

We are blind until we see
That in this human plan
Nothing is worth the making
If it does not make the man.

Why build these cities glorious
If man unbuilded goes?
In vain we build the work
Unless the builder also grows.

Whatever I ask of tomorrow, this above all I must demand. I must insist on a *quality* of life. The proudest achievement of technology will not do it. A resurgence, a recovery, of the life of the spirit is the *sine qua non* of human existence.

I must have God again as a child has his father. I must have this earth, this universe, again as a possession given me by my father. I must have my brother again, not as a rival to crush but as a brother indeed to love and care for.

And this is no illusory hope. God has gone to the length of a cross to make it possible. He is on the side of life abundant for me. He has assured me that since he has begun this plan of recovery, he has every intention of completing it. It will take him beyond my death to do it. Not until death is done with me and he has put me on my feet again on the other side will the task be completed. But God is on the way and there is no stopping him. There will be a recovered tomorrow, a glorious one, for anyone who lets him in.

I APPLAUD TECHNOLOGY

With this concentration on the life of the spirit, I need not hold the triumphs of science in disdain. I believe that every discovery is a gift from God, to be an ingredient in the abundant life. It should be just as possible for me to have a fullness of an inner life when I ride in a jet as on the back of a donkey. And have not the amazing scientific advances in medicine made it possible for a man to enjoy and exploit the abundant life the more and the longer?

The victories in technology have been so rapid and

so dramatic that we fear them. They threaten us with volcanic changes. Voices of doom are the fashion of the day. Instead of embracing these new discoveries as God's gift and invitation to a better day, we are overwhelmed by their possibility for destruction. We are almost ready to disclaim them as evil.

This is unworthy of a child of God. Did he not give to man a probing mind? Did he not include these secret resources in his creation? Must he not be pleased when his children uncover the riches he has placed within their reach? Must he not hope that they will have the spiritual wisdom and strength to harness them all for the more abundant life? And like an eager father, does he not stand ready to give us every possible help in achieving these ends, his ends?

I stood one day in the laboratory of a scientist who with stars in his eyes predicted what our new sources of power would achieve for man. He pointed out that with this power we could change salt water into fresh water in any quantity, and pump it through conduits to any part of the world. The Sahara desert, larger than the United States, could bloom like the rose, and all the arid regions of Asia could be gardens.

As a child of the God who holds these resources before me, can I do other than exult in the possibilities? Must I not cheer every new advance in knowledge as another evidence of the love of God for his children?

As a child in a small Dakota town I had no electricity, no running water, no radio, no automobile, no refrigerator. In the winter we melted snow on Sunday night for the Monday wash. We bathed on Saturday night in a wash tub on the kitchen floor. We had but a weekly newspaper. A blizzard might keep the train from reaching us for two weeks. I would not like to go back to "these good old days." I embrace the advances in technology with distinct pleasure! I want them to be a part of my tomorrow.

Swift as the changes have been, I do not renounce them. I know of no invention or discovery that I would like to surrender, except perhaps the bomb. Even this however, in the power it represents, could prove an asset.

As I write this, three of my countrymen are speeding at 4000 miles an hour toward the moon. Soon they will be a quarter of a million miles from the earth. I may have trouble justifying the expenditure of almost a half a billion dollars for the expedition, but I cannot but exult in the curiosity and the courage that lured a Leif Ericson to North American shores centuries ago and now entice his descendants into outer space. This is God's universe, and he has put it in the hearts and minds of men to explore it.

GOD IS ABROAD

Whatever confidence I have for the tomorrows will have to come less from my reliance on the ingenuity of men and more from my trust in God.

I know he wants me to have a future. And he wants it to be full and rich. He is far less concerned about the additional gadgets I may command than about the inner quality of my life, however. And I know that if death overtakes me, or overtakes the planet itself for that matter, it is not the end. God has a trump card. He has other islands in this vast archipelago where he will have me take up life again, and on a far more exciting scale. There are eternal tomorrows for me.

But I do not give up on the planet too easily. Until the Lord comes himself to usher in the final, consummate new order, I believe he has prospects of unpredictable possibilities on this earth. The earth is the Lord's. This is my father's world. He has not abandoned it, nor does he intend to do so. In unseen but powerful ways, he is still in command. He will keep seedtime and harvest, spring and fall, day and night going on schedule. He will keep the stage set for the drama of man's inner life.

Moreover, he is on the side of an abundant life for man. Christ announced that he had come to the earth precisely that man might have such a life.

In his incomparably beautiful *Rubaiyat* Omar Khayyam says,

Ah, Love, could thou and I with Fate conspire
To grasp this sorry Scheme of Things entire,
Would we not shatter it to bits and then
Re-mould it nearer to the heart's desire!

It has been shattered to bits with the coming of our Lord and the ushering in of the Kingdom of God. Into our present and into our future there has come a new dimension. Never again can we reckon the future without the miracle of God's presence. He is in our midst, nudging, prodding, and luring us on into a newness of life which alone makes any future desirable.

It is when I rest back into the assurance of his presence that I pick up courage. Paul's bracing words become mine: "What then shall we say to this? If God is for us, who is against us? He who did not spare his own Son but gave him up for us all, will he not also give us all things with him?"

The future is wide open. It is gloriously unpredictable, because our Lord is there.

THE HIDDEN DIMENSION

The tomorrow I want, therefore, is a life with God. It is a life with all the riches that only God can provide. Without him, even if I were to stretch my years to one hundred, or the planet to another million, life would be flat and finally intolerable. If not intolerable, at least a bore or a distraction.

C. S. Lewis points out that three things are necessary to the success of the voyage of a fleet of ships. First, every ship must be ship-shape. Second, the ships must not collide. But even if every ship is ship-shape and every ship stays in formation and does not collide with any other, there still is a third condition. The fleet must reach the destined harbor. If the voyage were ticketed for Liverpool and instead of reaching Liverpool the fleet ended up in Rio de Janeiro, the entire enterprise would have miscarried.

If we could organize society's future so that the entire world would have enough to eat and enough to wear (no one in want, everyone ship-shape), and if there were no wars or disorders (no collisions), mankind would have missed its total destiny if man had not reached God. It is life with God, and all the attendant qualities that such a life would give—it is this life which alone warrants a tomorrow.

In the parable of the Prodigal Son, suppose the son had "made it" in the far country, away from home and his father. Suppose he had invested in the right stocks and bonds, instead of squandering his money, and had become the tycoon in the far country. And suppose the story had ended with the entire country honoring him at some banquet, everyone fawning over him. This would be the model of our "success" stories.

In God's book, this would be a tragic plot. Whether the son ended in the pig sty as in the biblical account or on Park Avenue and Wall Street, the outcome would be equally tragic. For, in either event, he no longer shared life with his father. He was gone from home.

If the fondest dreams of utopia could be realized, it would not be enough. If the social planners could eventually eliminate war and hunger and cancer, and if every person on earth could be educated to enjoy music, literature, and science, the entire human enterprise would have miscarried if man no longer lived in fellowship with God. The angels in heaven would weep over a humanity lost.

In all our secular literature, God is a forgotten ingredient. Our analysts imply that if we could solve the massive problems of war, hunger, overpopulation, disease, and unemployment, our tomorrows would be secure. It would not be enough! We would live on this earth as in a vast orphanage, with every physical and even esthetic need satisfied, but orphans still. And in the spirit of man there would be a deep homesickness. There would be the longing and yearning for something more, something else. For man was made to live with God, and nothing less than God will do.

THE NEED FOR MYSTERY

Life with God yields a whole new world, the world of the spirit. All the laboratories of the world cannot touch this strange and wonderful existence.

It is a life of mystery. Beyond the known or the knowable! Mystery is something other than the yet unconquered. Once we knew little or nothing about diphtheria and polio. Now we know, and we no longer fear them as mysteries. Once the moon was a mysterious "lesser light," and now we walk on its surface. Science keeps pushing out the boundaries of knowledge, removing one mystery after another.

But the great mystery of God, the God who is above all and in all, this remains the unknown to science. If eventually science should know all about the far-flung bodies of this universe, including those bizarre bodies called the quasars, we would still face the rhapsodic mystery of God. Man needs this, if his spirit is to soar as it was designed to do.

Some years ago a popular song had this refrain, "Every little breeze seems to whisper Louise." To the lover, everything reminded him of his beloved. To someone not a lover, a breeze would be only a breeze, a movement of air to analyze. The analysis might be ever so thorough, but there would be little ecstacy.

To the person living in fellowship with God, everything whispers "God." Behind the wheat that grows, there is God. Beyond the sun that shines, there is God. The colors of the rainbow are more than a phenomenon of refracted light; they tell of the faithfulness of God. The birds that sing, the waves that roll upon the shore, the mountains that reach to the heavens—everything tells of him who created all things and who sustains them.

Remove God, and you have lost capacity for genuine wonder and awe. Lose this, and you have lost life. Without it, it matters little whether there is a tomorrow at all.

And I see God in you. This is the most important discovery of all. You are not a blob of protoplasm, a complex network of desires and appetites. You are more than the son of your father or a citizen of your country. You are the focus, the dwellingplace, of God. He is everywhere, to be sure, and in everything and beyond everything, but he has chosen you and me to be his singular habitat.

This makes all the difference in the world. You cannot treat me simply as a human animal anymore, nor can I dismiss you simply as a fellow traveler on this earth. You and I are sons and daughters of God. We are "fearfully and wonderfully made," as the Scriptures describe us. The mystery of God is in us. I stand in wonder and awe as I face you.

Think for a moment what this awareness can mean for the relationship that man will have with man. Every retarded child, every despairing person, everybody of any color or race—everybody becomes a mysterious representative of God to every other person. If I want to worship God, I must do it through you. I may sense God in the twinkling stars, but much more in the laughter of a child or in the sobbing of its mother.

I AM SOMEBODY

I was born in the first decade of this century. I have watched its brave hopes for man disappear. The optimism of the first years have, through two great wars and the unleashing of the bomb, given way to a heavy mood of pessimism. We speak of man's tenure on the earth having run out. Like the dinosaurs of old, man too may soon depart this planet.

The reason for this dark mood lies largely in our self-assessment. We have forgotten to remind ourselves that we were created to live with "the angels and the archangels and all the company of heaven." We have let ourselves be no more than the cousins of the dinosaurs. We have let go of God.

There is no way for me to recover my divine self-respect and therefore my hope for the tomorrows than to be recaptured by God. To take inventory of the triumphs of man is proving to be inadequate. In fact, our youth has turned its back upon history as nothing more than a record of man's failures, and in consequence is floundering for want of some ground to stand on as it faces the future.

There is no other place to stand than "the faith once delivered." I must stand in awe over against myself. I was created in God's image. I am given the strange and unique gift of freedom, the quality which is God's alone. I am given assurance of God's unconditioned and limitless love of me through the cross of Jesus Christ. God gives himself *for* me. I am the sort of creature that is more important to him than the entire planet. He did not die to recover the Pacific Ocean. He died to recover me!

Not until we stand here—in this faith—can we hope

to generate much enthusiasm for any tomorrow. Standing anywhere else, we will join the pathetic refrain of Macbeth, "Tomorrow and tomorrow and tomorrow creeps in this petty pace from day to day, to the last syllable of recorded time. And all our yesterdays have lighted fools the way to dusty death. Out, out, brief candle. . . ."

With the eyes of faith we can see in the yesterdays the repeated and continuing mercies of God. He who led Abraham out of Ur, he who rescued his people from Pharaoh, he who sent his son to save, and he who has promised never to leave us or forsake us, he walks with us still. In all our yesterdays God has been a light in the swirling darkness. Jesus Christ, the light of the world, in John's words "is still shining in the darkness, for the darkness has never put it out."

My hope for tomorrow lies here. I want to believe that God is not finished with this world. His kingdom is in our midst. And with God all things are possible. My grandchildren may live in a world of such plenty and peace, a world so afresh with a sense of God's love and with love for the brother that all other ages will fade into the shadows by contrast. I want to hold fast to this unpredictable prospect.

I know, of course, that if disaster overtakes us, this is not the end. If evil brings sufferings and chaos on a catastrophic scale, even then nothing can rob me of my birthright as God's child unless I turn from him. Death, the last enemy, cannot triumph over my resurrected Lord.

The maid, working in the home of Ralph Waldo Emerson, one day on the streets of Boston heard a street preacher say that the world would come to an end in two weeks. Unnerved and frightened, she hurried home to tell Mr. Emerson. She asked "What shall we do?" He replied, "Don't be so distraught. If it becomes necessary, I think we can get along without this world."

We can. There is another kingdom awaiting us when death can do no more.

But I like this world. It has much beauty. God has many bridgeheads for his mercy here. He has not abandoned it. He is at work in us and among us. Quietly and almost unnoticed, he is working miracles among us. We may be standing on the brink of a day when much of what he intended from the beginning will be recovered for us.

O God, give me a tomorrow, here and hereafter forever!

NOBODY

CHAPTER SIX

I WANT TO BELONG

Some years ago in Hartford, Connecticut, a huge circus tent caught fire. Scores of lives were lost. The charred bodies were at last identified—all but one. A little girl was unclaimed. They buried her in a hillside cemetery, and someone penned this epitaph:

There she lies as no one still,
Nameless on a lonely hill;
And the snowflakes and the rain
Come and go and fall again
On little Miss Nobody.

It's tragic not to belong to anyone, to be claimed by no one. We all belong to God, of course. He has claimed us by creation and again by redemption. But we need to belong to each other. I have need of you, and you have need of me. We cannot live in a continuous rendezvous with God, elemental as that need is. We must find horizontal ties as well as vertical. In fact, our Lord gave us no option. He said it was nonsense to lay claim to loving God if we did not also love our neighbor.

We are charged with being a very materialistic society. We boast of our gross national product and imply that this is the measure of our national greatness. Men buy newspapers and hurriedly turn to discover what the stock market has done. We are fascinated and enraged by reported salaries of notable people. We assume that money is power because money can command things.

Basically, none of us is controlled by things, unless we have surrendered our elemental humanity. A business man engaged in competition for profit will probably have on his desk a picture of his wife and their three children. If one day he receives a telephone call telling him that they were all killed in an accident, suddenly the entire meaning of his struggle for profits is gone. He sits at his desk with no reason for going on. It was people, his people, not profits, that gave life its meaning.

Because we struggle with a deep self-centeredness, we are tempted to use people. Then people, too, become things, pawns on a chess board to move about for our own advantage. But this is a distortion. The title of a book popular a generation ago, *How to Win Friends and Influence People,* had this cynical touch. I make you my friend in order to increase my sales or to win votes or to increase my prestige.

This is not belonging to one another. There may even be a mutual gain in our relationship, but we still do not belong. We hold one another at arm's length. If I cannot use you any longer or you me, we are done with one another.

TO BELONG IN LOVE

Belonging to one another ultimately means that we are tied together in love. You love me. That means that you have reached out to claim me, not to use me, but to serve me. And man needs desperately to belong—in love. This is what gives him his sense of importance. He is a *somebody* because he is loved by someone. He cannot become a *somebody* in any other way. He may gain the power of a Napoleon, the wealth of a Rockefeller, and the knowledge of an Einstein—but if he is unloved, if no one claims him in love, he will flounder. He has no identity without love.

A girl goes to college. She wants to be somebody. She tries the usual techniques. She dresses well, she spends hours before the mirror, she studies hard, she woos the best societies or clubs. And she is in competition with every other girl who is trying the same methods.

Then one day a boy falls in love with her, let us say the quarterback on the football team, the president of his class, the most popular man on campus. Suddenly she is a *somebody*. She is loved. No longer does she engage in this frantic competition for importance. She is important. She belongs! She is the loved one.

Psychologists and psychiatrists are unanimous in diagnosing most of man's ills as a want of belonging to someone in love. "I Can't Give You Anything But Love, Baby," may be a rather insipid ballad, but to give everything but love is as tragic as the ballad is frivolous. Security does not come from wealth or power. Security comes from love.

And love is never a tool, never a means to an end. Love is an end in itself. Our Lord taught us that! He does not love us in order to save us or to change us. He saves us, because he loves us. If he never succeeds in changing us or saving us. he loves us still.

He commands us to love one another, and he adds, "Love is the fulfilling of the law." It is the ultimate. He does not tell us to love our fellowmen in order to lure them into heaven, or to change their way of life. Whether love achieves anything or not, we must love. For that's the nature of his love.

Kierkegaard, the great Danish theologian of the nineteenth century, declares that if a woman were to marry for any reason other than love, she would debase love. If the gods were to promise that if she married she could become the mother of the savior of the world, and she were to marry for that reason, she would have betrayed love.

THE MANY CIRCLES

I want to belong. To whom? In my more expansive moments I may say that I want to belong to everyone, everywhere, to the whole human race. And this is the terrifying dimension our Lord holds before us. All men are my neighbor, and I am to love my neighbor as myself.

The orbits of my belonging are many, however, and they are like concentric circles. I have a family—a wife and children and grandchildren. I belong to them in a singular way. The accident of birth has given me a small, tight circle as a kind of laboratory where I learn what it is to love and be loved, what it means to belong.

But I am not to remain in this circle alone. A family can become in itself a very self-centered and ultimately an unwholesome clique. Once when Jesus was informed that his mother and brothers were waiting for him, he made what seemed a calloused reply, "Whoever does the will of God is my brother and sister and mother." Whatever his subtle meaning may have been, he was indeed expanding his "belonging" to a larger circle than his immediate family. It is tragic when we fail to move into the larger circles, and belong only to small cells—our family, our nation, our race. We do belong to mankind, difficult as it is to stretch our boundaries. Our heavenly father is the father of all. His family, and therefore our family, circles the globe.

But we dare not minimize the small circles. The laboratory of the family is of extreme importance. A man who has learned to love his brother may far more easily learn to love a stranger, and make him his brother. And may it not be that he who has learned to love his own country may the better become an internationalist? To love in the larger circles does not mean that we abandon the smaller. We move to the larger precisely because we have learned to belong in the smaller.

THEY ARE MINE

There is something exhilarating about the use of the first person singular, or plural for that matter: *my* country, *our* country. And there is something shameful about saying, "The country is going to the dogs." Whose country? I like it when a man says *my* country, *my* club, *my* congregation, *my* world. He belongs. He identifies with its weakness and its strength. He assumes responsibility. It is his.

For years at Christmas time I took time to read Dickens' *Christmas Carol* to my children, until we got a recording of Lionel Barrymore's reading of it. It never failed: when we got to the part where old Scrooge faced Jacob Marley's ghost with the plaintive defense "But you were always a good man of business, Jacob," I was always thrilled with Jacob's response, "Business, mankind was my business, charity, mercy, forbearance, benevolence were all my business . . . the dealings of my trade was but a drop of water in the comprehensive ocean of my business." And later in the story when Scrooge himself rejoined the human race to belong to all men, most of us had to wipe away a tear.

I had a father like that. For 46 years, morning, noon, and night, he walked the same two blocks between his home and the village store. Once a fire destroyed his building. Otherwise he turned the same key in the same door, lived with the same neighbors, served the same customers, came home to the same wife. For 36 of those years he had the same pastor. His life may have seemed uneventful, a dull routine. But he belonged. He belonged to the community and the community belonged to him. And upon his death there were neighbors, customers, salesmen, and competitors who recounted incidents which some facile writer could have woven into an epic.

It is when *belonging* leaps over one circle after another to encompass all within reach that life takes on its intended meaning.

THE GREAT COMPANY

In one of the great creeds of Christendom, confessed by the church the world around, we say, "I believe in one, holy, Christian (catholic) and apostolic Church." It is in the sweep of this affirmation that the state of belonging takes on its fullest and richest sphere. Nothing can compare with the depth and height of this circle. Sometimes we call this the Kingdom of God. This is a belonging that defies the limits of death itself.

The simple statement, "I belong to the church," should send us soaring.

We who belong to some congregation have done this rapturous kingdom a great injustice. We have allowed ourselves to become little, local "in-groups" with bickerings and jealousies. Sometimes we have degenerated into smug, defensive cells, singing with self-righteous priggishness,

> *How blessed is the little flock*
> *Whom Jesus calls his own,*

and have forgotten the strident phrase of our liturgies, "Therefore, with angels and archangels and all the company of heaven we laud and magnify thy glorious name."

For these two thousand years the church of Jesus Christ has been the one strident company. "Crowns and thrones may perish, kingdoms rise and wane." The church goes on. Attacked and derided as it is today in many parts of the world, it remains still the one orbit, the one community, which can elicit from the heart of man the deepest loyalties, the widest love, and the highest hope. It is the one group which anchors me in time and in eternity. When I belong there, I belong forever!

The 20th century has been called the "ecumenical century." Beginning with the International Missionary Conference in Edinburgh in 1910, the Christian denominations have struggled with the relationships of the churches within the one church. Christ has only one church; this we all confess, whether we are dubbed Lutheran, Episcopalian, Catholic, or Presbyterian. I may have some "local" pride in being Lutheran, but it is my membership in the one, holy church that holds me captive.

Let me try an illustration. A man from India visits the United States. As his guide and host I take him on an extensive tour through the fifty states. The tour completed, he says, "I have now seen the separate states; now show me the United States of America." At this point I cannot very well take him to the District of Columbia and say, "This is the United States." Neither the White House nor the Capitol building is the United States. Nor is it just the collection of the states. For the great nation which is called the United States of America is a kind of "hidden" legal and cultural reality which includes and encompasses all the states but is also something "more" or "other" than a mere collection of states. And any state, to be a worthy part of the United States of America, must in its own government and life express the greater "governmental" reality which is the whole.

To belong to the United States I must also belong to one of the states. In some such way I have membership at one and the same time in one of the denominations and in the one, holy, Christian, and apostolic Church. When I say "my church," I may simultaneously be speaking of my congregation, my denomination, and the one holy, catholic, and apostolic church. I belong to all three. I have loyalties to all three. But it is to the Lord of all three that I really belong and to whom I have the elemental loyalty.

Again, let us ask, "What is the church?"

The church is not a building.
Nor is it a book.
Nor is it an altar.
Neither is the church an organization.
Nor is it a denomination.
Nor is it a fraternity of priests or ministers.
The church is a people.
It is the people—or the family—of God.
They belong—belong to God and to one another.

This fellowship is the profoundest of all. It is stronger than family or country. It leaps over all boundaries. Most of us who belong fail to grasp the epic sweep of its reality.

We belong to Jesus. This is the key. We are in him and he is in us. If I am in him and you are in him, this knits us together as cells are forged together in a body, or as separate branches are together on a common trunk. We have no choice. We are one. The only possible way for me to be rid of you is to be rid of Jesus. If I separate myself from him, I can separate myself from you. There is no other way for us not to belong to one another.

Even if I don't know you, I belong to you. I may enter a church on Sunday morning and take my place among strangers. But we are not strangers. I sing the hymns with you, pray the prayers with you, listen raptly to the same gospel with you, confess my sins with you, affirm the faith with you. I may leave the church service not having shaken hands with anyone. But I have been in the presence of my brothers and sisters in the Lord. We belong to one another, because we belong to him.

Of course I need to know you, as many of you as possible. And I need to be drawn into intimate association with some of you, so that we can indeed bear one another's burdens, weep with those who weep, and rejoice with those who rejoice.

THE RIGHTS I CLAIM

If I ask, "What do I have a right to expect from my church?" I have certain obvious claims to make.

I have a right to be given the Word of God and the Sacraments. These are the means, or channels, through which God the Holy Spirit conveys knowledge, comfort, and power. In fact, God comes to us through these instruments. If on a Sunday morning my pastor has been distracted into discussing some contemporary issue and has overlooked giving me the glad, good news that in Christ I have the forgiveness of sins and the assurance of a life everlasting, I feel cheated. I need to be exhorted to the good life, but I need to be reminded that I hold my rights to the kingdom of God not through an inventory of my performance, but through the gracious work of God for me.

I have a right to be deeply disturbed. If I am ushered before God, which the church should do for me, I cannot expect to be complacent. The expectations of the kingdom should be so vividly presented that I am left crying, "God, be merciful to me, a sinner."

I have a right to be encouraged and prodded. The glorious assurance of forgiveness should be ringing in my ears. The right to begin each day anew, without dragging along the rubbish and debris of the past, should be made clear. The style of life which our Lord gave us while on earth should haunt me and lure me on. I should leave the church with the praises of God echoing in my spirit and with firm resolutions to try harder anchored solidly in my will.

I have the right to be filled with gratitude. Even if my path is littered with pain and sorrows, I should have a continuing and pervasive gratitude—because the love of God has been rhapsodically proclaimed in the cross, the guarantee of the constancy of God's love.

And I have a right to be turned from myself to my brothers!

OUT FROM GRATITUDE

Gratitude to God is the only power comprehensive enough and sustaining enough to enable a man to turn from himself to his brother. It is the key to all ethical questions. Our problem is not primarily to know what is good. Our problem is to find something which will make a man *do* the good when he knows the good.

Of course there are difficult areas. We face new ethical questions every time we expand the boundaries of knowledge. But we have the Scriptures, we have conscience, we have the experience of the race, and above all we have the command to love.

But it is gratitude to God for his love that drives us on to find ways to thank him for this love.

He has made this task both easy and difficult. He has said that whatsoever we do to the least of these, our fellowmen in need, we have indeed done it for and to him.

We who belong to him, we who have been baptized into Christ, we who are members of the one holy church —we now are plummeted into all the world. Our brothers are not only those who are brothers in the faith, fellow members of the Church, but every man, woman, and child on the earth, whatever faith or no-faith they may have. If we had ever had the delusion that we could confine ourselves to the "in-group," the church, this is utterly shattered. He has returned us to mankind. We belong to everyone. All have a claim on us. He has given us no other way to thank him but to serve our brothers.

It no longer matters whether our neighbor is black or white or yellow. It is quite irrelevant whether he likes us, wants us to help, or rebuffs us. It is not a question whether our efforts may achieve anything or not. We are under higher orders. We must set out to love, to work for mercy and justice, to try and try and try, come what may. We are not drawn to men's hurts primarily by their cries for help; we are propelled from above. God has loved us and made us heirs of his kingdom. Our response is to thank him our whole life through, and the only channel he has given for our gratitude is service to our brothers.

As a young man in Parliament, Sir William Wilberforce had a decisive encounter with God, a conversion if you will. For a time he thought to leave Parliament and enter into "religious work," when his friend, the Younger Pitt, persuaded him to remain in government and work against the slave trade, the cancer of the empire. Years later when his hair was turning white, Wilberforce met with Parliament one evening to have the issue of slavery settled.

A member of Parliament closed the address of the evening with these words; "I am thinking tonight of two heads and two pillows. One is the head of Napoleon, tossing feverishly on a pillow on the island of Helena, after having left a trail of blood from Jena to Waterloo. One is the man who tonight will see the consummation of his life's work. If I were to choose, I would not choose the pillow of Napoleon; but the head that will rest tonight, after our vote is taken, on the pillow of Wilberforce."

In countless less dramatic instances in thousands of communities life has been made better for millions of people through the efforts of men and women who have set out to thank God by turning to the work of mercy and justice for their brothers. These are the people who belong, who belong to God, who belong to the one, holy church and who through that belonging also belong to all men.

Enthralled with the principle of the lever and its fulcrum, a man made the extravagant boast, "Give me a place to stand and I will move the world." If we are to move the world, if we are to give mercy and righteousness the sturdy stuff that will keep going in the face of all vicissitudes, we will have to find a place to stand *beyond* and *apart* from this world. We must start with God. Propelled by gratitude to him, in this gratitude we may take on the world. There is no power for good afoot on this planet to compare with this. It is much more than sentiment. It goes far beyond the desire or need to survive.

Through his incredible love I have been reclaimed for his kingdom. I am a prince in his royal house. I am a son in his family. Under him, I am a manager of this earth and a co-worker with him in the enterprises of love, mercy, justice, and joy.

FOREVER AND EVER

And when death comes, I still belong. My life is not bounded by the moment of birth on the one hand and the caprice of death on the other. Death is but the briefest of interludes. He who raised up Jesus from the dead stands ready to put me on my feet again and commission me to a life of service and joy without end on the other side.

We end the words of the Nicene Creed with this triumphant affirmation, "I look for the resurrection of the dead; and the life of the world to come." To describe this life is beyond the power of words, except to say what obviously it is not. It will not be a life of hatred, fear, pain, or tears. It will not be a state of oppression or greed. All the distressing limitations which plague our world will be gone.

Even in moments of high ecstacy or great contentment, how many of us do not feel a longing and a yearning still —a loneliness, a lurking melancholy—as if we were yet reaching for something unattained?

Nothing on this earth can set all the strings of a man's heart singing. For man has been created to live in untroubled and unrestrained fellowship with God, with the angels and archangels and all the saints. This joyous company and life can be seen and known on earth only as through a veil.

When death comes, then the struggles of the church militant will subside and the children of God will stride into the halls of the triumphant church assembled around the throne of its Lord, there to belong to him and to one another forever.

Alvin N. Rogness is president of Luther Seminary, St. Paul, Minnesota. As a parish pastor, retreat leader, churchman, and popular speaker, he is known by many as a spiritual counselor in the style of C. S. Lewis. Among his books are *Captured by Mystery* and *Forgiveness and Confession*.